TERRIFIC TOYS

TERRIFIC TOYS AND HOW THEY ARE MADE

By Noah Leatherland

KidHaven PUBLISHING

Published in 2025 by
KidHaven Publishing, an Imprint of Greenhaven Publishing, LLC
2544 Clinton St., Buffalo, NY 14224

Written by: Noah Leatherland
Edited by: Rebecca Phillips-Bartlett
Designed by: Amelia Harris

Cataloging-in-Publication Data

Names: Leatherland, Noah, 1999-.
Title: Terrific toys and how they are made / Noah Leatherland.
Description: Buffalo, New York : KidHaven Publishing, 2025. | Series: Terrific toys | Includes glossary and index.
Identifiers: ISBN 9781534547100 (pbk.) | ISBN 9781534547117 (library bound) | ISBN 9781534547124 (ebook)
Subjects: LCSH: Toys--Juvenile literature. | Toy industry--Juvenile literature.
Classification: LCC GV1218.5 L438 2025 | DDC 790.133--dc23

Manufactured in the United States of America

CPSIA compliance information: Batch #CSKH25: For further information contact Greenhaven Publishing LLC at 1-844-317-7404.

Please visit our website, www.greenhavenpublishing.com.
For a free color catalog of all our high-quality books, call toll free 1-844-317-7404 or fax 1-844-317-7405.

Find us on

Image Credits

All images are courtesy of Shutterstock.com, unless otherwise specified. With thanks to Getty Images, Thinkstock Photo and iStockphoto. Cover – Ganna Demchenko, Nadiia Korol, Will Thomass, Anna Kaminska. Used on all pages – Shmelkova Nataliya. 2 – Kolpakova Daria, Monkey Business Images. 4 – StockImageFactory.com. 5 – Emese, Mcimage. 6 – David Leshem. 7 – Zyabich. 8 – lovelyday12, Carlos andre Santos. 9 – Proxima Studio. 10 – pogonici, Watercolor_ Art_Photo. 11 – Florida Chuck, mdbildes. 12&13 – Mauro Rodrigues. 13 – Prokrida. 14 – Sergey Ryzhov. 15 – Alexandra Morosanu. 16 – FabrikaSimf, Monkey Business Images. 17 – Frame Stock Footage. 18 – Hodoimg, asharkyu. 19 – Larina Marina, Kyrylo Glivin. 20 – Kolpakova Daria. 21 – Jeanette Virginia Goh, KaliAntye. 22 – StepanPopov, Photo Oz. 23 – Ilina Yuliia, Brookhaven National Laboratory (BNL) [Public domain].

Contents

Words that look like this can be found in the glossary on page 24.

Terrific Toys

Toys are things that you use to play. Toys bring lots of fun, but where do they come from? These toys did not just appear. They were made somewhere by someone.

What is your favorite toy?

Making Toys

There are lots of different types of toys and games.

They all get made in different ways. Some ways of making toys have existed for hundreds of years and some are new.

Made by Hand

Toys have been made for thousands of years. Today, most of our toys are made with machines.

Before these machines were **invented**, humans had to make toys by hand.

This toy is thousands of years old!

The oldest toys were made from anything people could find, such as rocks, wood, and plants. Even though people have invented lots of clever machines, some toys are still made by hand.

Wonderful Wood

Wood comes from trees. First, a tree needs to be cut down.

The logs from these trees are then chopped into smaller pieces. Toy makers cut and **carve** these pieces into shapes.

Once the wooden pieces have been carved into shapes, they are painted and put together. Toy makers might need to use glue, or the pieces might fit together just right!

Do you have any wooden toys?

Soft and Stuffed

From teddy bears to dolls, soft toys can look like anything. First, a **pattern** needs to be drawn. The shapes of that pattern are drawn onto big sheets of **fabric** and cut out.

Lots of different fabrics can be used to make soft toys.

The fabric pieces get **sewn** together to make the shape of the toy.

The toy gets filled with fluffy stuffing to make it soft. Now, the soft toy is ready to play!

Metal Makers

Metal toys are made in a few ways. Some metal toys are made by cutting out parts on a thin metal sheet. These parts are bent into shape and put together to make a toy.

Bending metal is the oldest way to make metal toys. Toy makers have found lots of new ways to make metal toys.

Metal can also be melted and made into new shapes to make toys.

Plastic Pieces

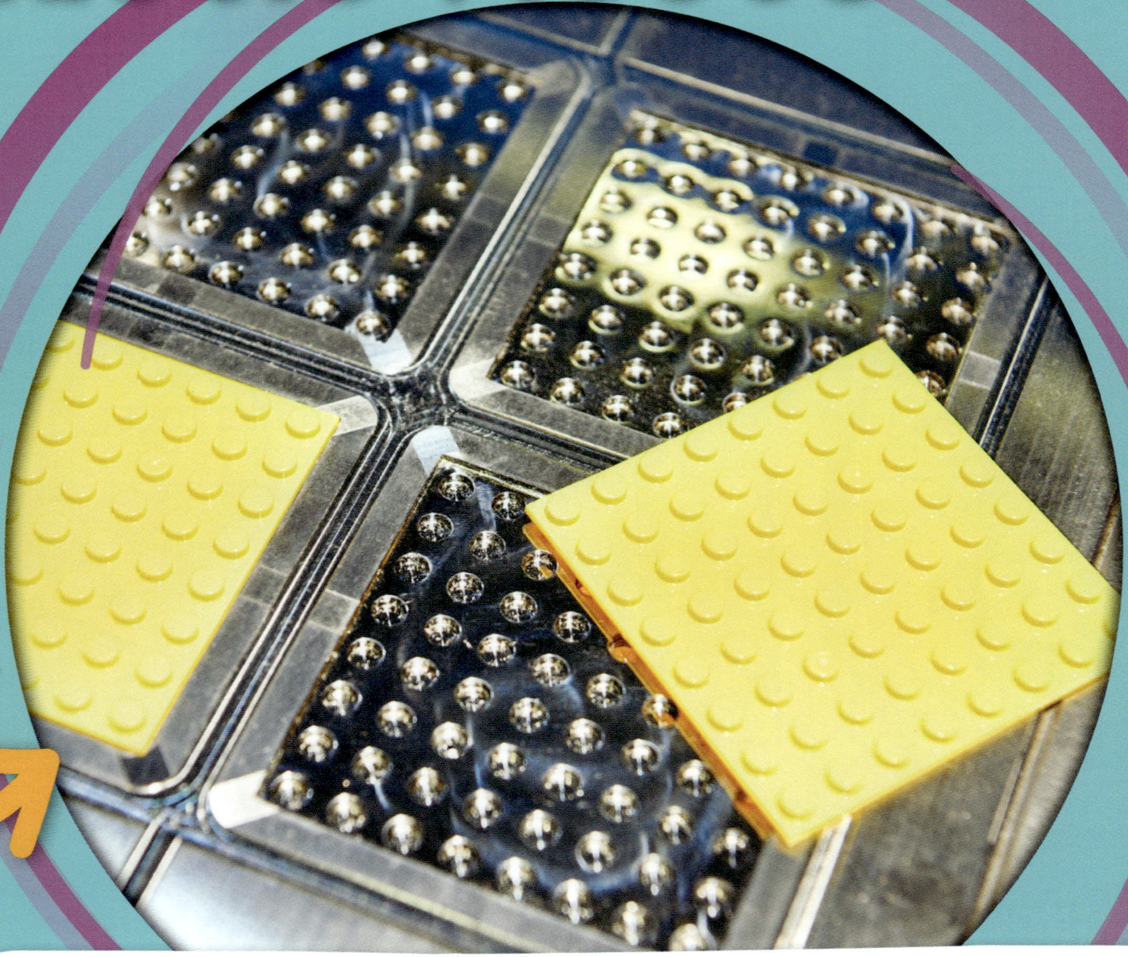

Plastic toys are made using a **mold**. First, small pieces of plastic are melted down into a **paste**. Then, the melted plastic is poured into the mold.

The plastic stays in the shape of the mold when it cools down. The plastic is taken out of the mold, ready to be put together. These pieces can make all sorts of toys.

Factories can make thousands of the same toy using molds.

Vivid Video Games

Lots of video games are played on a machine called a console. Inside of these consoles are lots of computer parts. The games themselves are **digital** and are made on computers.

Video games can be made by one person or hundreds of people.

There are lots of steps to making a video game. Using computers, video game **designers** plan how their games will look, sound, and play. It can take years to make one game!

Do you have a favorite video game?

Printing Toys

A new way to make toys is using a 3D printer.

A 3D printer is a machine that can make three-dimensional shapes, such as cubes and spheres. These are shapes that can be held in your hands.

As well as simple shapes, 3D printers can print all kinds of things.

Some people use them to print different plastic parts that can be made into toys.

Make Your Own!

There are many different ways to make toys and many different **materials** to make toys from. You do not need machines or tools to make your own toys!

You can make toys out of different materials you can find at home. All it takes is a little imagination!

What could you use to make a terrific toy?

Fun Facts

LEGO makes more tires than actual carmakers.

Some of the earliest toys in history were made of stone.

Some toys get made by accident! Play-Doh was made to clean walls!

The first video game was made in the 1950s.

Glossary

carve to cut a hard material into a shape

designers people who plan how something should be made

digital showing information as an electronic image

fabric a material made by weaving threads of cotton, wool, nylon, silk, or other materials

invented when something new is made

materials things from which objects are made

mold a container with a certain shape that liquids are poured into

paste a thick, soft substance

pattern a design used as a guide

sewn joined pieces together using thread and a needle

Index